For Lisbeth Ellen Sarah Redfield, reader.

With thanks to the knowledgeable and enthusiastic children's librarians of the North Vancouver District and Vancouver public libraries.

Visit us on the World Wide Web at www.groundwoodbooks.com

Groundwood Books / Douglas & McIntyre
720 Bathurst Street, Suite 500
Toronto, Ontario M5S 2R4

Distributed in the USA by Publishers Group West
1700 Fourth Street
Berkeley, CA 94710

We acknowledge the financial support of the Canada Council for the Arts, the Ontario Arts Council and the Government of Canada through the Book Publishing Industry Development Program for our publishing activities.

Canadian Cataloguing in Publication Data
Ellis, Sarah
The young writer's companion
A Groundwood book.
ISBN 0-88899-411-7
1. Creative writing — Juvenile literature. 2. English language — Composition and exercises — Juvenile literature.
PE1408.E47 1999   j808'.042   C99-932056-4

Printed and bound in China
by Everbest Printing Co. Ltd.

The
Young Writer's
Companion

SARAH ELLIS

BLUE BIRD

A GROUNDWOOD BOOK

DOUGLAS & McINTYRE

VANCOUVER TORONTO BUFFALO

INTRODUCTION

When I was a kid I made up stories all the time. Some of these stories were fantasies and mostly they started, "When I have a horse ..." Some of the stories were about revenge. They often starred Shirley, a big mean girl in grade six, and described how I would scorn her when I was a rich, famous, glamorous grownup. I had a whole collection of stories about an invisible fairy called Peter who went with me everywhere and said encouraging things when I was scared or hurt. And then there was the series of tear-jerking tragedies in which I was a very brave and cheerful disabled orphan.

I also made up stories with my friends as we played. One day we were heroic veterinarians, operating on our stuffed animals and bringing them back from the brink of death. The next we were a band of girl detectives, gathering clues and outwitting the police. In the kitchen we were inventors, making perfume or new kinds of sandwich spread. (We never did find a market for pre-mixed peanut butter, mayonnaise and banana.)

I made up stories all the time, but I never once thought that these imaginings had anything to do with the kind of stories you wrote down. When I was asked to write a story in school, I didn't have a single idea. I would just stare bleakly at the blank paper. Sometimes I tried to copy the kind of story I liked to read — a gang of kids having an adventure — but I always seemed to get my characters stuck in a cave somewhere and then I couldn't think what to do with them.

I was a reluctant writer.

Now that I am an unreluctant writer, I am often asked where I get my ideas. I love this question, and I like to ask it of other writers. What I've discovered is that writers get their ideas in a huge variety of ways, and many, many writers keep a notebook to jot down these ideas.

Everyone who plays, daydreams, reads, thinks, listens and talks has ideas all the time. *The Young Writer's Companion* gives you some suggestions — my own and those of other writers — on how to grab those ideas as they fly by.

You can use this book in many different ways. Start a journal or a masterpiece, make lists and doodles, use it as a scrapbook to collect clippings, neat words or headlines. Store your ideas until one day, faced with a blank piece of paper or an empty screen, you can take them out and let them grow.

Sarah Ellis *is the author of several award-winning books for young people, including Governor General's Award winner* Pick-Up Sticks *and* Out of the Blue, *winner of the Mr. Christie's Book Award. Sarah lives in Vancouver, British Columbia.*

Islands in the Mind

Robert Louis Stevenson was a strange little boy. He was so skinny that people said he looked as if his bones would poke through his clothes. The damp climate of his Scottish home made his weak lungs worse, and he was sick more often than he

was well. An only child, he never attended school regularly and, apart from his cousins, he had few friends. If you had seen him sitting in an Edinburgh park — pale, weak and overprotected by his stern nanny — you might have felt sorry for him.

Yet inside his head, Louis had a rich, exciting life. He could make a whole world out of anything — toy soldiers, Bible stories, tales his nanny told him, his own terrifying nightmares. He could even make a world out of his breakfast.

When Louis and his cousin Bob had breakfast together, they made kingdoms in their porridge. Bob sprinkled sugar on his porridge and explained how his kingdom was a harsh northern land covered with snow. Louis poured milk on his porridge to make an island with bays and coves — an island in terrible danger of being swamped by the milky sea.

Years later Louis was doodling one day with some watercolor paints. On his paper appeared an island. Something about the shape of his doodle delighted Louis, and he started to imagine the characters who lived on this island and the adventures they might have.

So began a furious fifteen-day writing frenzy in which Louis wrote the first fifteen chapters of *Treasure Island*, a pirate adventure story that has been enjoyed by readers for more than one hundred years.

DRAW AN ISLAND

Doodle an island. Goof around with the shape until it pleases you. Now you have the outline of a whole world and a bunch of questions.

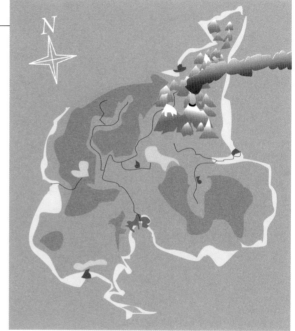

• Are there hills, valleys, plateaus, mesas, mountains? Are the mountains volcanic? Is the terrain steep or gentle? Are there beaches, cliffs? Draw in these features.

• Are there rivers? Are they wide and lazy or dangerous with white water and rapids? What about lakes, swamps or marshes? Maybe there is quicksand.

• Name the features of your island. This is a good chance to make up words. If you need a jump-start, browse through the index of an atlas. While you've got the atlas handy, check out some geography words like firth, estuary, bight, sound, isthmus. (Revenge possibility: Name a mosquito-ridden pestilent bog after someone who is bugging you.)

• Is the weather cold or hot? Dry or wet? Windy or still? Moderate or extreme? How many seasons? Is there rain? Snow, hail, fog? Where do the winds come from? Are there droughts, storms, hurricanes, tornadoes?

• Plants, insects, fish, reptiles, birds and mammals? Real or invented?

At some point your island will start to seem real to you. That's a good time to visit it. Pull your canoe (raft, rubber dinghy, rowboat) onto the shore; moor your sailboat (submarine, hydroplane, yacht) or find a landing place for your helicopter (dirigible, fighter-bomber, bi-plane). Get out and take a walk.

What do you smell? What do you hear? What does the air feel like? What are the colors of your island? Do you feel safe here? What's that movement just around the curve in the path?

If you walk around your island you will find a story. It might be action-packed like *Treasure Island*. It might be quiet or funny or just plain weird. Maybe you'll encounter some people. Maybe you'll turn into a different person yourself. You might write the whole thing down at once, or you might tuck parts of it away in your head or your notebook for later.

If you get stuck or tired take a break. After all, you just created a whole world.

When Maurice Sendak was nine years old, he got his first real book as a present, *The Prince and the Pauper*. First he stared at it. Then he smelled it. Then he tried to bite it.

When Lloyd Alexander was a kid, he loved to eat the food mentioned in whatever book he was reading. His mother did the best she could. For the nut-brown ale and venison steaks in *Robin Hood*, she gave him ginger ale and a hamburger.

Robert Louis
Stevenson never went
anywhere without two
books, "one to read
from, one to write in."

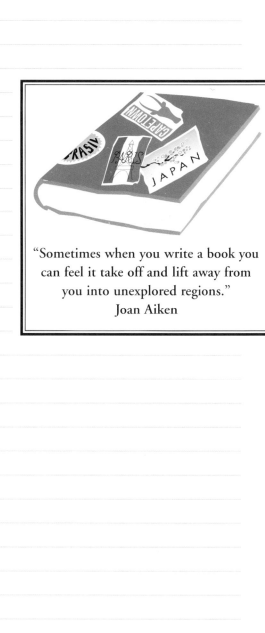

"Sometimes when you write a book you can feel it take off and lift away from you into unexplored regions."
Joan Aiken

"I thought
The Yearling was the
most wonderful book
I'd ever encountered. It
made me want to be a
boy; I wanted to be
poor and live in a
swamp, where I would
have animals as
friends."
Lois Lowry

AN ARCHIPELAGO OF ISLAND BOOKS

Brink, Carol Ryrie. *Baby Island*.
Two sisters shipwrecked on an island with four babies. Now that's a babysitting challenge!

Cole, Brock. *The Goats*.
Laura and Howie, marooned on a small island without their clothes, are the "goats," victims of their fellow campers. How do they survive and keep their dignity?

Fry, Rosalie K. *The Secret of Roan Inish*.
Fiona's baby brother was swept out to sea in his wooden cradle, but there are rumors that he is still alive.

LeGuin, Ursula K. *A Wizard of Earthsea*.
Sparrowhawk is a young wizard in training on the island of Roke. He is talented but foolish, and one day he unleashes a terrible power.

Macken, Walter. *Island of the Great Yellow Ox*.
Two boys and a toddler encounter a couple of villains who will stop at nothing in their quest for an ancient treasure.

MacLachlan, Patricia. *Baby*.
When the summer visitors leave Larkin's island, a baby is left behind.

O'Dell, Scott. *Island of the Blue Dolphins*.
Twelve-year-old Karana is abandoned on a Pacific island by her tribe.

Paterson, Katherine. *Jacob Have I Loved*.
Twin sisters growing up on a small island. Caroline is beautiful and gifted, destined for great things. But what of Louisa? What is her destiny?

Paulsen, Gary. *The Island*.
Will's life is going down the toilet until he discovers the island.

Seabrooke, Brenda. *The Bridges of Summer*.
Zarah finds out a lot about her heritage when she visits the island home of her grandmother, the daughter of slaves.

Steig, William. *Abel's Island*.
Like any castaway, Abel must find food and shelter. Unlike most castaways, Abel is a mouse.

Taylor, Theodore. *The Bomb*.
Sorry Rinamu's Pacific island home is threatened. What can one sixteen-year-old boy do against the U.S. atomic weapons testing program?

Family Stories

It is Sunday afternoon. Jean Little's normally hectic house is quiet. Her father and brothers are outside playing. Her mother is curled up in a chair reading.

Five-year-old Jean feels like a story. Not just any story. Her own story.

She picks up her baby book, an album of photos and notes, and creeps up onto her mother's lap.

"What does this say?" she asks, pointing to the first page of the album. Her mother smiles. Jean has already heard this story many times before, but she needs to hear it again.

Her mother begins. "It says you weighed seven pounds, six ounces when you were born ..." Jean snuggles in for the rest of the familiar tale of how she couldn't see as a baby, but then one day she reached for a spoon and her mother, realizing that Jean did have some vision, cried for joy.

We all need family stories — the familiar stories of who we are and where we came from. Jean was lucky. She grew up in a close family with aunts, uncles, cousins, a grandmother — all willing to talk about their interesting lives. Jean tucked these stories away in her memory, a savings account of family history.

Years later, she mastered the art of shaping family stories into fiction. She used the events of her own life — her early childhood in Taiwan, her move to Canada, the experience of feeling excluded, living with a disability, her place in her family — as the emotional heart of her novels. She learned to shape and embroider the past by "adjusting" facts, inventing people, joining bits and pieces together to make a coherent story.

COLLECT A FAMILY STORY

Family stories are the icing on the family cake. They are fun. They connect you to your relatives. They give everybody a chance to show off.

Family stories are especially valuable to the writer. Stories that are told over and over again and are passed from person to person get better with each telling. By the time you hear a family story, it has already been polished and edited.

You probably already know family stories. The time Uncle Mark crazy-glued his glasses to his nose. When Judy mislaid the baby. The mysterious wedding guest. Caitlin's horrible job interview. The worst landlord in the world. How we finally found cousin Bruce's pet rat.

Sometimes people need encouragement to remember and tell family stories. A well-timed question at a family party, on a boring bus ride or while you're doing the dishes can often get things started.

Was anyone in your family ever the victim of a crime? Ever in a flood? Ice storm? Tornado? Ask your parents how they met. Ask about the day you were born. Ask how your name was chosen.

- What is something I have in my life that you didn't have when you were a kid? What is something you had that I don't have?

- What were you afraid of when you were little? What was the scariest thing that ever happened to you?

- Did you have a pet? Do you remember the day you got it? Who named it? Why?

- What were you not allowed to do when you were a kid?

- What was your best moment at school? What was the worst?

- Did you have a secret place as a child?

- Did you ever go to emergency, have an operation, wear a cast?

- What was the worst thing you ever did when you were a kid?

- What did you do that your parents never knew about?

- What was the most amazing coincidence you can remember?

- Did you ever have a weird neighbor?

- Did you move often? Houses, cities, countries? What was the best thing about the new place? What did you miss the most about the old?

> "When I started
> writing I wanted to
> share some of the
> things our parents
> shared with us when
> we were little."
> Michael Kusugak

Lois Duncan's first stories were a series of disaster tales invented in the dark to give her little brother nightmares.

Johanna Hurwitz in a library: "I suddenly realized that I would never live long enough to read all the books that were waiting for me. It was a wonderful yet terrible discovery."

"Some days I'd borrow three titles (the maximum allowed) from the town library, read them, and get them back to the library by five o'clock, in time to exchange them for three more before the library shut."
John Marsden

> "Writing is like baseball or piano playing. You have got to practice."
> Betsy Byars

"Learning to write is like doing scales for fourteen years, except you don't know you are doing them."
Rosemary Wells

Family stories make a great addition to any writer's notebook. They don't need to be long or dramatic. Collect small incidents and details. As Jean Little says, "Always, for me, it is one small story that pulls me into writing a longer one."

Cresswell, Helen. *Ordinary Jack.*
The Bagthorpes are a talented family. They win prizes, medals, cups and certificates in swimming, karate, music, languages, electronics. Except for Jack, that is, eleven years old and ordinary. This is the story of Jack's hilarious quest for a place to shine.

Doyle, Brian. *Up to Low.*
When young Tommy and his dad go off to the farm at Low, they enter a world of family. There are great-grandparents, grandparents and more aunts and uncles than you can keep track of. There is the neighbor family, Mean Hughie, and all those kids. And don't forget the red-headed Hendricks. Tall tales rule.

Enright, Elizabeth. *The Saturdays.*
One wet boring weekend the Melendy children form the Independent Saturday Afternoon Adventure Club. By pooling their four allowances, one of them gets to do something really great. And the others? They occupy the afternoon by doing something free, like inventing a cure for measles, or burning down the house (by mistake, of course).

Estes, Eleanor. *The Moffats.*
Jane hides in a box for a day to avoid a run-in with the chief of police. Rufus loans his precious tooth collection to improve the Halloween pumpkin. Joe teaches a dog to dance. Times are hard in the town of Cranbury and the Moffats are poor, but they never fail to have a good time.

Garnett, Eve. *The Family from One End Street.*
There are a lot of Ruggles and their life runs from calamity to calamity. Lily Rose and the ironing disaster, Jim and the Gang of the Black Hand, John's ill-fated money-making scheme, baby William's quest for fame. It all adds up to one of the happiest families between two covers.

Gilbreth, Frank. *Cheaper by the Dozen.*
The true (well, more or less) story of a family of twelve kids and their eccentric father. Mr. Gilbreth believes in efficiency in all things. The efficient bath (learn a foreign language while you get clean), the efficient dinner (learn times tables while eating), the efficient tonsil operation? Family life at its most uproarious.

Nesbit, E. *The Story of the Treasure Seekers*.

When the Bastable family finances reach a crisis, the six Bastable children do the sensible thing and look for treasure. When traditional methods such as digging don't work out too well, they try solving crimes for the reward and selling poetry to newspapers. Then there's always finding a wealthy princess to marry or kidnapping somebody. The Bastables are not easily discouraged.

Streatfeild, Noel. *Ballet Shoes*.

Great-uncle Matthew progresses from collecting fossils to collecting orphans. Pauline is rescued from an ocean liner that hit an iceberg. Petrova is found in a hospital. Posy is the gift of an impoverished young dancer. The living Fossils create an unusual family, especially when they take a vow to become famous.

Taylor, Sydney. *All-of-a-Kind Family*.

Five sisters all dressed alike. They are poor in money but rich in stories, adventures and celebrations. Their father's junk store is an Aladdin's cave of delights. Purim, Passover and the Fourth of July are opportunities for feasting and visits. And then something happens that makes them not quite all of a kind.

Waterton, Betty. *Quincy Rumpel*.

The Rumpels are a family with lots of ideas. The Rumpel Weed-Puller, the Rumpel Hygienic Toothbrush Holder, Rumpel Rebounders, mushroom growing, doorknob collecting. This spirit of do-it-yourself includes the kids. Ear-piercing, hair cuts, hair permanents? Why not just do it at home? There's never a dull moment when Quincy and her family are around.

Waugh, Sylvia. *The Mennyms*.

The Mennym family lives in a large house in London. The grandparents work at home. Father has a night job. They worry about money. The baby takes a lot of care. The teenage daughter is a bit rebellious. They could use some friends. But they don't mix with their neighbors. They can't. They have a secret. The Mennyms are a family of life-sized, animated, stuffed dolls.

Monsters from the Deep and Other Imaginary Beings

Moving day. Groan. All that stuff. For most of us, moving day doesn't happen too often. For Michael Kusugak, growing up in the far north, moving was a way of life. For the first six years of his life, Michael lived in the age-old Inuit tradition of traveling. The family traveled by dog-team in search of whales, seals and cariboo. In winter they lived in igloos. In summer they pitched a tent. The nomadic life is not a life for collecting possessions. The family had only the essentials — furs, weapons and tools. But they also had something that required no space and had no weight, but which was essential to their survival. They had stories.

Small Michael would fall asleep every night listening to the stories of his parents and grandmother. Legends, family stories, funny stories, stories with something to teach. He heard tales of the animals he knew — the bear, the cariboo, the squirrel. And he heard stories of imaginary beings.

When Michael grew up, he remembered a story told in the spring. In the far north spring can be a dangerous time for children as the sea ice begins to break up. To keep their children away from the hazardous shore, parents tell stories of the

Qallupilluit, a witchy undersea creature who kidnaps children. In *A Promise Is a Promise* (written with Robert Munsch), Michael Kusugak invents his own version of the Qallupilluit and puts it into the world where he lives now — a world of jeans, TV and computers.

CREATE YOUR OWN CREATURE

Try creating your own imaginary being. Describe and/or sketch it. Here are some hints to get you started.

• Try beginning with a creature you've already heard of. The tooth fairy, Santa's elves, the Easter bunny, Ogopogo, the abominable snowman, the gremlin that caused your hard drive to crash, your little sister's imaginary friend. Expand and embroider this creature until you have made him/her/it your own. What does it look like? Where did it come from? What does it want?

• You can also invent an entirely original creature, cooked up from scratch. To start, take an ordinary human being and change one element such as:

Size: tiny people or giants

Color: neon orange skin, yellow eyes, green fingernails

Feelings: the boy who didn't know what fear was, the girl who couldn't feel pain

Extra abilities: flying, invisibility, shape-shifting, animal communication, extra-acute hearing, ESP, immortality

Needs: the man who never slept, the woman who lived on water and air

Habitat: underground, undersea, the people of the clouds, sewer-dwellers

• Name your creature. Imagine how it talks. Pretend you are it and write down your feelings and your impressions of the world. Design clothes for it. Draw floor plans of its house.

• If you live with your creature for a while, stories will begin to happen. Does your creature have a problem? Enemies? Does it remain entirely in its own world or does it interact with humans? Perhaps you are the human it meets.

If your story bogs down, don't try to think up more plot. Instead, go back to your creature and hang out a while longer. Ask more questions. After all, nobody knows more about this creature than you do. It came from inside your head.

When Michael Kusugak was young, his soccer field was a huge winter field of sea ice. Sometimes families would gather and play soccer all night long.

The language of the Inuit is Inuktitut. In this language the word for the Northern Lights means the trail of light that ball players make in the sky.

"I didn't want to be a writer. Writing seemed boring. You sat in a room all day by yourself and typed."
Betsy Byars

Cooper, Susan. *The Boggart*.
An ancient, invisible, mischievous creature is transported from his castle home in Scotland to Toronto. The modern world gives him plenty of scope for creating mayhem. Don't miss the scene in which he gets involved in a hockey game.

Kendall, Carol. *The Gammage Cup*.
The Minnipins live in Slipper-on-the-Water, in the Land Between the Mountains. Their life is peaceful, safe, steady and, let's admit it, boring. All this changes when they are threatened by their old enemies, The Mushrooms. Unearthing ancient armor, village upstarts lead their neighbors into victorious battle. Who are the Minnipins?

MacDonald, George. *The Princess and Curdie*.
Curdie is a miner. He knows how to deal with the goblins that inhabit the underground world. But deep in those dark places live other creatures — horrible half-human, half-animal beings like Ballbody and Legserpent. MacDonald creates some of the most nightmarish inventions to be found in fiction and then makes us care about them.

Mayne, William. *Hob and the Goblins*.
Hob takes care of things in the house. "He tidies away abandoned things, like scraps of quarrels or pieces of spite. He banishes small troubles, makes ghosts happy, soothes tired curtains, charms kettles into singing, and stops milk from sulking." Hardly anyone can see Hob, but he is a very useful creature to have around. His abilities are stretched to the limit, however, when he has to deal with goblins. Meet Hob and you will never forget him.

McGraw, Eloise. *The Moorchild*.
Saaski is a changeling, half-fairy and half-human. Rejected by the village because she is different and unable to live with the fairies because she doesn't have all the fairy skills, she doesn't fit in anywhere. This moving book is for anyone who ever felt they didn't belong.

Norton, Mary. *The Borrowers*.
Have you ever wondered what happens to lost paper clips and thumb tacks and the last piece of the jigsaw puzzle? They have probably been borrowed, by the miniature people who live under the floorboards.

From Journal to Fiction

Thurs. 14th, 1843 — Mr. Parker Pillsbury came, and we talked about the poor slaves. I had a music lesson with Miss P. I hate her, she is so fussy. I ran in the wind and played be a horse, and had a lovely time in the woods with Anna and Lizzie. We were fairies, and made gowns and paper wings. I "flied" the highest of all.

This is a page from the journal of a ten-year-old who loves to play and make-believe and dress up. A reader and a writer named Louisa May Alcott. At this point in her life she and her family are living at an experimental farm commune near Boston. The members of the commune are very strict. No meat, cold baths, long discussions about serious issues. It's true that there are acres to run in, trees to climb, and her sisters and neighbors to play with. Children are treated with respect, asked their opinions, invited to join in discussions. On the other hand the food is very boring — apples, bread and potatoes, over and over again. And there are too many adults around, butting in, expecting you to be good — adults like the dreadful Miss P.

Worst of all, Louisa's parents are always arguing. She hears her mother crying at night. There is no money for the mortgage or for food. The crops are not thriving, and Louisa's mother wonders how they will make it through the coming winter.

The Alcotts, like any family, are a mixture. There is love and irritation, good times and disaster, harmony and tension. And Louisa records it all in her diary.

By the time Louisa was thirty-five years old, she was a hardworking professional writer. She had published stories for magazines, articles for newspapers, plays, fairy tales for children and a novel for adults. She was the chief financial support for her parents and sisters, but money was still a problem. One day a publisher friend asked her to write a "nice book for girls." Louisa thought no one would be interested in such a book, but she wrote it anyway.

Never was a writer more wrong. *Little Women* was a runaway success. It made Louisa May Alcott a famous woman, and a rich one.

In writing *Little Women* Louisa May Alcott invented a whole new kind of book — a family story with realistic people, a story that concentrated on the small details of everyday life. For material she simply used her own family, transforming the Alcott family into the March family. She turned herself into Jo, the energetic, impetuous and passionate heroine of the novel, and everyone's favorite character.

Louisa May Alcott had had years of practice in describing everyday life. In her daily journal entries she had been storing away a rich treasure-house of material — the events, celebrations, frustrations, joys and tensions of a real family. She wrote *Little Women* in just eight months. But really Louisa May Alcott had been writing this book her whole life, in her diary.

LIFE ON THE PAGE

The garbage dumps of the world are full of diaries that only contain three entries — January 1st, January 2nd, January 17th and that's it. What's to say, right? Got up, had Shreddies, went to school, did paper route, watched TV, went to bed. Your pencil grinds to a halt.

If you are a lapsed diary writer, or if the thought of keeping a diary makes your brain go numb, perhaps you have a limited idea of what a diary can be. Some people enjoy keeping a record of the facts of their daily lives — what they ate, the weather, what came in the mail, the bank balance. But there are also many other kinds of diaries.

A Trip Diary
Buy a nice notebook for your next holiday. Holidays are good for diary writing because there are lots of new things to see and experience. You also often have more time for writing when you're on holidays. And a trip diary makes a better souvenir than those plastic totem pole salt and pepper shakers.

Sorting Out Feelings
A diary makes a good friend when you are miserable. Lucy Maud Montgomery once wrote that if it were not for her diary, into which she could spill her feelings, she would have become sick with worry and frustration. Sometimes writing about your problems helps

you discover what you should do. More often it helps just to write it all down. Diaries are a safe place to get angry, to cry, to complain, to be afraid. They don't get hurt feelings and they don't tell secrets.

The Commonplace Book
Heard a good joke lately? Found an article on your favorite singer? Come across a song lyric that really

hit you? Got a postcard of a painting that you'd like to save? A program from a play? Found a line in a book that you would like to remember? A collection of bits like this is called a commonplace book, a scrapbook of stuff you like. Add your own comments, too. This book will be uniquely your own.

As someone once said, "Creating a book is too good an idea just to be left to writers."

A Grab Bag of Diary Ideas
Weather, emotions, opinions, resolutions, ambitions, dreams, family stories, gossip, quotations, your own poems, lists, fantasies, jokes, names, interesting words and phrases, things you want to find out about.

For starters, why not just try a list? Ten favorite words. Five truly boring activities. Three good things about being oldest, youngest, middle or only. Three bad things about same. Seven uses for snow.

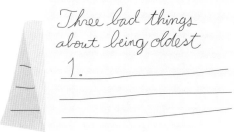

(A final liberating hint about diaries: You don't need to do it every day.)

Louisa May Alcott once met Charles Dickens, whose books she loved, but she didn't like him much. She thought he was a show-off. Sometimes it's better not to meet your favorite writers!

> "I didn't know that average people could be writers. I thought you had to be a genius, born with a quill pen in your hand."
> Sid Fleischman

"I am an accomplished eavesdropper — in restaurants, trains, and gatherings of any kind."
Rosemary Wells

Every story Roald Dahl wrote started out as a three- or four-line note in the worn-out school exercise book he kept as a journal.

Like many women writers, Louisa May Alcott planned her stories while doing chores. "I can simmer novels while I do my housework."

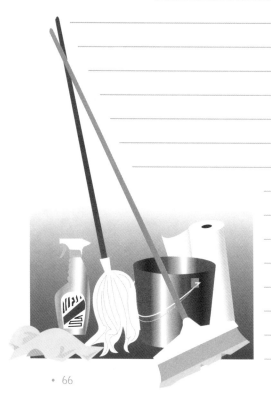

"I think I shall write books, and get rich and famous: that would suit me, so that is my favorite dream."
Jo in *Little Women*

Blos, Joan. *A Gathering of Days*.

The year is 1830. Catherine is thirteen years old but in her world she must act as an adult, keeping house for her widowed father and younger sister, helping with the running of the farm and dealing with a new stepmother and a runaway slave. Her journal is our window on her world.

Cleary, Beverly. *Strider*.

In his diary, fourteen-year-old Leigh Botts tells the story of joint custody, of a dog that Leigh shares with his friend Barry. A dog can be a big help when you are having a fight with your friend, when your dad loses his job or when you say something really stupid to a girl you like.

Cushman, Karen. *Catherine, Called Birdy*.

"There was a hanging in Riverford today. I am being punished for impudence yet again, so was not allowed to go. I am near fourteen and have never yet seen a hanging. My life is barren." Birdy's diary, written in 1290, reveals the frustrations of a lively girl who sees life passing her by.

Fitzhugh, Louise. *Harriet the Spy*.

Harriet is in training to be a writer. She observes the world around her and records her observations in a Spy Notebook. But when her school friends find the notebook, Harriet gets into deep trouble.

Gantos, Jack. *Heads or Tails: Stories from the Sixth Grade*.

Jack has a creative approach to what you can keep in your diary. He keeps baseball cards, his stamp collection, photos, fortunes from fortune cookies, squished bugs and, oh yes, these very funny stories from his life.

Hest, Amy. *The Private Notebook of Katie Roberts, Age 11*.

Katie's notebook is the friend to whom she tells her feelings about her new stepfather, her move from New York City to Texas, her need for a best friend and her big plan for getting her old life back.

Jones, Robin D. *The Beginning of Unbelief*.

Hal begins this journal to get rid of somebody. The somebody is his childhood imaginary friend Zach. As Hal pushes Zach deeper and deeper into the science-fiction universe he has created in his journal, the events of Hal's own life start to make sense.

Sterling, Shirley. *My Name Is Seepeetza.*

Twelve-year-old Seepeetza is two people. At the Indian residential school she is Martha; at home on her family ranch she is Seepeetza. These two selves come together in her journal, where she reveals the miseries of school, the fun of summer holidays and the joyous escape of reading.

Townsend, Sue. *The Secret Diary of Adrian Mole Aged 13 3/4.*

In his diary Adrian reveals himself to be a deeply sensitive poet-in-the-making. The trouble is that nobody notices. Not his parents, not his friend Nigel, not Pandora of the beautiful hair, not even his dog. Only his diary knows the real Adrian Mole.

Real-life Journals

Filipovic, Zlata. *Zlata's Diary: A Child's Life in Sarajevo.*

When Zlata begins her diary at age ten, life is ordinary. She writes of family, school, sports and the Madonna fan club. But then the bombs begin to fall on her home city of Sarajevo. Zlata lives through the pain and fear of life in a war zone and records her feelings in her diary.

Frank, Anne. *The Diary of a Young Girl.*

This document of a young Jewish girl in hiding from the Nazis during World War II is probably the most famous diary of all time. That this book was rescued is a kind of miracle. Reading it makes history real and now.

Hunter, Latoya. *The Diary of Latoya Hunter: My First Year in Junior High.*

This real-life diary, written over one school year, is a document of changes. In twelve-year-old Latoya's life in New York, the events in her external world — travel, becoming an aunt, witnessing a crime — are mirrored in the growth she is experiencing in thought and spirit.

Parry, Caroline. *Eleanora's Diary.*

The journal of a pioneer girl beginning in 1833, when Eleanora is ten years old. The voyage from England to the new world, a visit to a circus, funny comments about her family, descriptions of pets, silly poems and great little doodles make Eleanora's diary a delight to read.

Clip and Write

It is a warm, showery June evening in 1905. A woman named Maud is sitting at the kitchen table. She is thirty years old and a writer. She has already published articles, poems and many short stories in magazines, but her life is difficult. She lives with her demanding and grumpy grandmother. Maud often feels frustrated, especially in the winter when cold weather traps her inside.

But now it is spring, and Maud's spirits rise. She is excited about the blossoming trees, and about the prospect of starting a new story. She browses through her notebook — an ideas book in which she jots down bits of description, plot and character. She comes across the following, a note she made from a newspaper story:

"Elderly couple apply to orphan asylum for a boy. By mistake, a girl is sent them."

With this plot snippet, Maud begins to write. What appears on the page is a girl called Anne, a red-haired orphan who is high-spirited, imaginative and a non-stop talker. She tells the truth with gusto and she gets into a lot of trouble.

It quickly becomes clear to Maud that Anne is too big for a short story. Anne needs her own book.

Anne of Green Gables is now famous worldwide. The book and its sequels have been translated into many languages. Anne has been transformed into a play, a musical, a television series, a doll. Thousands of tourists visit Prince Edward Island every year to see Anne country. In Japan there is a whole theme park devoted to *Anne of Green Gables*. Anne is mega. And the person who was Maud to her friends and family is L.M. Montgomery to us, her readers.

Where did this book come from? The character of Anne certainly came from L.M. Montgomery herself, and the places in the book were the scenes around Maud's real home. But the seed of the book — the one little plot idea that got the whole thing cooking — came from a newspaper clipping.

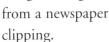

FOUND STORIES

Reading like a writer makes reading the newspaper a whole new experience. Once you've read the comics and checked out how your favorite team is doing, browse through the rest of the paper. Pay particular attention to the little articles — the pieces that fill in the spaces between the "real" news of taxes, crime and politics.

You may be handed a plot idea nicely served up on a platter.

Honolulu. A sixteen-year-old boy was found alive in a ravine six days after he fell 100 meters from a scenic lookout while climbing over a railing to get a better view. Gabriel Robinson was rescued by helicopter and taken to hospital in fair condition. He survived on only water from a stream. His parents thought he was staying with friends.

What would it be like to be that hungry? How would you try to survive? Were there any animals? If it was you, what would you think about in those six days?

Sometimes newspaper stories give you a single incident that could be part of a larger story:

About 100,000 pagers rang wild across the United States yesterday. The half-hour beeping spree was caused by a single wrong number punched into a computer system. A new customer was mistakenly given as his P.I.N. a code used to send news headlines. When that P.I.N. was activated it triggered beeps and messages all across the country.

What would happen if a similar error caused everybody to get the same message at the same time? What would it be like to be on a bus and have 27 beepers all go off simultaneously? Could some hacker pull this off as a practical joke?

*hool bars boy for wearing
ess to semi-formal

Zookeepers dress penguins in scarves during recent cold spell

Goat runs for mayor, is poisoned by political rival

Child needs therapy after Cabbage Patch Kids Snacktime doll gnaws hair

What kind of person would do that, and why?

Often newspapers give you great ideas for characters. Need some weird parents in your story? How about this couple?

Last year in Sweden, a couple was fined $735 for naming their son Brfxxccssmnpccclllmmmnprxvclmnckss qlbb11116 (pronounced Albin). They are surrealists, says Parade magazine, and wanted their offspring to have a name that was "full of meaning and typographically expressionistic."

Sometimes newspaper articles simply provide a jumping-off place for your own ideas:
Camels are fitted with tail lights in the Australian tourist town of Broome. The beasts, which carry tourists for sunset rides along the beach road, posed an unacceptable hazard to traffic. Tour operators agree to outfit their camels' rear ends with flashing, battery-operated bicycle lights.

What if pedestrian traffic got so heavy in cities that people had to wear turn signals and stay in lanes? What if you had to put money in a parking meter just to sit on a park bench? What if people started turning into cars?

Start your own clippings collection, ideas galore.

L.M. Montgomery loved reading "The Lady of the Lake." "I used to pore over it in the old schoolhouse when I should have been wrestling with fractions ... all the same, it did me more good than the fractions would have done. It was nourishment for the heart and mind and soul."

MEAN CHARACTERS

FUNNY CHARACTERS

MORE IDEAS

IDEAS

GRAB
BAG

"Everything I've ever felt, whether it's been good or bad at the time, has all contributed to the emotion that goes into my writing."
Gillian Rubinstein

"A sculptor may get metal or marble dust all over himself, and a painter gets pigment deep in the pores. I think a novelist gets this noise, this irritation, at the tips of the fingers. I need to type, to write with my hands."
Virginia Hamilton

"When I was nine years old I found an old typewriter up in the attic. I brought it downstairs and started typing stories and little joke books and magazines. I've been doing that ever since."
R.L.Stine

Bell, William. *Forbidden City*.
A Canadian teenager visits Beijing at the time of the Tian An Men massacre.

Dickinson, Peter. *Eva*.
Eva is the first of her kind, a thirteen-year-old girl living inside a chimpanzee's body. A highly original novel with some provocative things to say about overpopulation and humankind's assumptions of superiority.

Ho, Mingfong. *The Clay Marble*.
The author writes from her own experience to tell us the story of a twelve-year-old Cambodian girl who becomes a refugee.

Hughes, Monica. *Invitation to the Game*.
Imagine a society in which there is no work for those graduating from high school. Where will these young people find a sense of purpose, challenge, accomplishment and identity? In this science-fiction novel, they find it in The Game.

Katz, Welwyn Wilton. *Whalesinger*.
A fantasy novel in which a young woman communicates telepathically with a mother gray whale, this ambitious book also draws on the big news headline of 1579, when

Sir Francis Drake visited the coast of California.

Mahy, Margaret. *The Other Side of Silence*.
Hero, a child who does not speak but is a gifted observer, discovers the secret of the house next door and what it contains.

Marineau, Michele. *Road to Chlifa*.
The experiences of a young Lebanese man who leaves his wartorn country for Canada.

Temple, Frances. *A Taste of Salt*.
Contemporary war and conflict form the raw material for this novel about seventeen-year-old Djo, a young man caught up in the conflict in Haiti.

A Bag of Tricks

Ladies and Gentlemen! Presenting — the Master of Magic, the Captain of Conjuring, the Prince of Prestidigitation! Would you welcome please, the amazing ... ALADDIN!

The audience bursts into enthusiastic applause as a tall, thin teenager comes into the room. He is dressed in a long white robe and wears a brown wig. He carries a bag of tricks.

It is a winter's night in the north part of England one hundred and fifty years ago. In attendance is the large Dodgson family, seven girls and four boys.

Coins appear from behind the ears of the youngest children. A magic wand floats in the air. A piece of paper is transformed into a boat and then disappears into thin air. In the flickering light from the fireplace, the magician in his costume looks so mysterious that the audience almost forgets that he is their brother, Charles, the eldest son in the family.

Years later, Charles is a respected but shy teacher of mathematics at Oxford University, but he still likes to play and entertain. He is at his best with children, and he has many child friends. He carries a bag of tricks with him from which he produces candy, toys and puzzles of his own invention. But his best tricks have to do with words. Anagrams, puns, funny versions of popular songs, acrostics, riddles — Charles is a word magician.

One afternoon when he is boating with a fellow teacher and three child friends, one of the children, Alice, asks Charles for a story. Charles invents a little girl called Alice who falls down a rabbit hole. The story includes songs, nonsense poems and brain-teasers, as Charles creates a topsy-turvy world where things stand on their heads.

Alice, in particular, loves this story. Over the next few months, Charles writes out the story by hand and adds his own illustrations. Then he gives it to Alice as a Christmas present.

When *Alice's Adventures in Wonderland* is eventually published, Charles Dodgson, the shy mathematician, chooses the pseudonym of Lewis Carroll. This is the name we remember. Alice has become the most famous children's book in the world, the favorite book of a wide range of people, from scientists to poets, from computer programmers to rock musicians.

Trick #1: Portmanteau Words

In Lewis Carroll's bag of tricks are many weird invented words. For example, he devised the word "slithy," which he explained as "lithe and slimy," and "frumious," a combination of "fuming" and "furious." These glued-together words are called portmanteau words.

Nowadays portmanteau words are all around us. Some are sensible and useful, like "brunch" (breakfast and lunch). Some are so familiar that we have almost forgotten that they are portmanteau words — "electrocute" (execute and electricity), for example.

Carroll, however, went in for portmanteau words that were not so much useful as funny. Put on a Carroll brain and try inventing a portmanteau word of your own.

Step One: Find a word you like. Flip through a dictionary if you need inspiration.

e.g., curmudgeon — a bad-tempered person

Step Two: Say the first syllable of the word to yourself. (Don't worry about spelling, just say the sound.)

e.g., cur

Step Three: Think of words that end with that sound.

e.g., soccer, hacker, sucker, faker

Step Four: Glue this word onto the beginning of your original word.

e.g., soccermudgeon

Step Five: Define your new word.

e.g., soccermudgeon — a grumpy soccer fan

glitterati infomercial guesstimate beefalo Muppet faddict neatnik mocktail lamburger Chunnel witticism happenstance scrunch splurge twiddle frabjous

Lewis Carroll would probably have loved computers and making
his own homepage. See what someone else has created for him at
http://www.lewiscarroll.org/carroll.html

POW

THWACK

'twas the fight before Christmas...

On top of Spaghetti, all covered with cheese,

I lost my poor meatball when somebody sneezed...

Mary had a little Spam...

Trick #2: Parody

A parody is a humorous, exaggerated imitation of a poem, song, character or writing style. When you sing, "I hate you, you hate me. We're a normal family" to the tune of the Barney song, that's parody.

Give parody a try. For inspiration think of the parodies you already know, such as the "other words" to Christmas carols ("Jingle bells, Santa smells, ninety miles away..." or "Joy to the world, the school burned down...").

Songs, ads, TV shows, your school's code of conduct, the rhymes you learned in nursery school, the national anthem, recipes. What happens if you keep the style (rhythm, rhyme, structure, melody) but change the content?

Parody is particularly suited to group invention and often happens when you're sitting around with friends feeling goofy.

"I collect words wherever I go and rejoice in their beauty or despair over their poverty."
John Marsden

Trick #3: Riddles

At the mad tea party the Mad Hatter suddenly asks Alice, "Why is a raven like a writing desk?" Alice is relieved. Now she knows what's going on. It's riddle time.

Riddles can be plain funny but they can also be used as weapons in a game of power, as in the riddle contest between Bilbo Baggins and Gollum in *The Hobbit*.

Riddles have to make sense, but not ordinary sense. Inventing and solving riddles involves making your brain jump sideways. Sideways thinking is a useful skill for a writer, and making up and solving riddles can put you in a writer state of mind.

Pun riddles, for example, are jokes for the ear, using pairs of words or phrases that sound alike or almost alike:

What do vampires have for dinner? Human beans.

What do you get if you put a canary in a blender? Shredded tweet.

What did one melon say to another? "I cantaloupe with you."

To make up a pun riddle, start with a sound-alike pair of words and then work backwards from the punchline. Hair/Hare. Play with "hair" — hairline, hair loss, hair piece, hairdresser. . .

Hairdresser. Hare-dresser.

Why did Beatrix Potter put Peter Rabbit in clothes? A: Because she was a hare-dresser.

(This is a space in which to groan, the usual response to pun riddles.)

For more riddles try
"Riddle du Jour"
http://www.dujour.com/riddle/

Inside Outside

You throw away the outside and cook the inside. Then you eat the outside and throw away the inside.

A: A cob of corn.

Juster, Norman. *The Phantom Tollbooth*.

Travel to the land of Expectations, Dictionopolis, the Word Market and the Castle in the Air. Meet the Mathemagician, Dr. Dischord, the Undersecretary of Understanding, the Whetherman and the lovely princesses Rhyme and Reason.

Lear, Edward. *A Nonsense Omnibus*. You probably know "The Owl and the Pussycat." Don't miss "The Jumblies," "The Pobble Who Has No Toes," and "The Dong With the Luminous Nose" — poems from the grandfather of nonsense.

L'Engle, Madeleine. *A Wrinkle in Time*.

Three beings from outer space — Mrs. Whatsit, Mrs. Which, and Mrs. Who — transport a trio of children to the planet Camazotz, ruled over by the dreaded and repulsive IT.

Mahy, Margaret. *Nonstop Nonsense*. Life in the Delmonico family becomes very strange when Mr. Delmonico offends the word-witch. While waiting for the Delmonicos to settle down we pass the time with the Wily Flingamango, the Dictionary Bird and others.

Sandburg, Carl. *Rootabaga Stories*. Did you ever hear about Jonas Jonas Huckabuck who had a job as a watchman watching watches in a watch factory? Do you know the romantic tale of How Two Sweetheart Dippies Sat in the Moonlight on a Lumber Yard Fence and Heard About the Sooners and the Boomers? Sandburg turns words into a fireworks display.

Thurber, James. *The Wonderful O*. Dastardly villains invade the peaceful island of Ooroo and proceed to destroy everything that contains the letter O. Confusion and chaos reign. What can the people do to defend their alphabet and their lives when their world is governed not by the letter of the law but by the law of the letter? Read this one aloud.

Wynne-Jones, Tim. *Some of the Kinder Planets*.

Kids named Cluny and Hezekiah. The mysterious alien message, "Save the moon for Kerdy Dickus." A little boy staring down a ground-hog hole. The spirit of Lewis Carroll lives on in these stories. Alice even makes a guest appearance in "Tweedledum and Tweedledead."

Yours Affectionately

*Dear Aunt Linda,
Thank you for the socks.
They are ~~nice interesting~~
different.*

Sigh.

You chew the end of your pencil.

You think about lunch.

You have to write a letter and you have

NOTHING TO SAY.

AAGH!

One day in 1893 a young woman named Beatrix Potter had this very problem. She wanted to write a cheery letter to a family friend, a little boy called Noel who was sick in bed. But what do you say to a five-year-old?

Beatrix Potter decided to tell Noel a story.

". . . I shall tell you a story about four little rabbits whose names were Flopsy, Mopsy, Cottontail and Peter. They lived with their mother in a sand bank under the root of a big fir tree."

The letter continued with the story of naughty Peter who disobeys his mother and goes into Mr. McGregor's garden and nearly gets caught but escapes in the nick of time. The story-letter contained all the things a little boy might like — being bad, delicious food, losing your jacket, and a chase scene.

Noel carefully kept this letter, which is lucky because seven years later Beatrix Potter asked to borrow it back. She had decided to try to publish Peter Rabbit as a book.

The Tale of Peter Rabbit has been around for nearly one hundred years. Your great-great-grandmother might have read it. It has been translated into a dozen languages from Icelandic to Latin. There are Peter Rabbit baby clothes, mugs, stickers, stamps, figurines, board games, posters, T-shirts and slippers. There is a ballet based on Beatrix Potter's stories and a movie made from that ballet.

And it all started with a letter.

WRITE A LETTER

Letter-writing is an excellent activity for all writers. Letters provide a place to try out words and ideas in a casual way. They give you an excuse for buying great stationery. And they give you a guaranteed audience for your work. Everybody loves getting letters.

If you have only ever written thank-you notes or letters home from camp, try some new letter-writing possibilities:

Find a pen pal
To find a pen pal by e-mail try "Keypals Club"
http://www.mightymedia.com/keypals/
or "Kidscom"
http://www.kidscom.com/orakc/pwdkeypal.html
or "Kids Space Connection"
http://www.ks-connection.com/

Write fan letters or letters to the editor
Do you have a message for your

favorite actor, writer or musician? Have they dropped your favorite strip from the comics page? Are there plans to close your local swimming pool? Do you have an opinion about acid rain or zoos or rollerblading  bylaws? Have your say. Get it off your chest. Make a difference.

Send postcards
Write postcards to your friends and relatives when you're away on vacation. Practice micro-writing. How much can you fit on one postcard? Stuck at home? Design and make your own postcards using collage,

painting, drawing or photos. Then pretend to be away in some exotic location — Argentina, Egypt in the time of Tutankhamun, Mars. Confuse your friends.

Story-letter relay

Start a story in a letter. Leave it at some cliff-hanging point and mail it to a friend to continue. Bounce

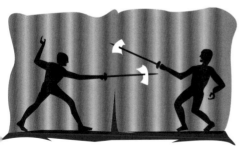

it back and forth. Just remember, as they say in Theater Sports, "No Blocking, No Wimping." (Blocking is finishing the story so that the other person has nowhere to go. Wimping is ignoring what the other person has added to the story.)

Letters from an altered state

Write a letter as though you are someone else. Pretend to be your hamster writing to his cousin describing his adventures in the hamster ball. Be an Olympic athlete e-mailing home on the eve of the medal competition. Compose a letter from an orphan to the parents he never knew. Write the letter that Rapunzel scratched on the walls of her tower. Pretending to be someone else and writing in that voice is what fiction writing is all about.

TO THE MANAGEMENT:
THE ACCOMMODATION
YOU HAVE PROVIDED
LEAVES MUCH TO BE
DESIRED — R

"A letter is so much better than a phone call. It is there in the middle of the night if I want to reread it. It is there a week or a month or a year later if I want to recall what was said to me."
Johanna Hurwitz, who had five penpals when she was in junior high school

Letter Writing TIP #1 • Write as if you are talking

Listen to what's going on in your head and then write it down. C.S. Lewis, writing a thank-you letter to a little girl called Sarah, wonders why he can only draw a cat from the back, and further, why people's faces are so much easier to draw than animal faces.

Letter Writing TIP #2 • Use detail

A small thing described in detail is more interesting than a big thing described in a general way.

In a letter, Beatrix Potter describes her discovery of a nest of 79 snail eggs. She says that they were white, just like breakfast eggs, except that they would be just the right size for mice.

Letter Writing TIP #3 • Trivia rules

Don't restrict yourself to "important" things.

Rudyard Kipling, writing to his son, devoted several lengthy paragraphs to an accident in which he cut his finger. No gory detail omitted.

Letter Writing TIP #4 • Be immediate

What's going on right at the moment you're writing the letter?

Lewis Carroll was sitting on the beach on a windy day, writing to his sister Mary, when he noticed a mother and child passing by, the mother holding the child's head. Carroll interrupts the subject of his letter to speculate that perhaps the mother was trying to prevent the child's head from being blown off.

Letter Writing TIP #5 • Doodle, draw and decorate

Beatrix Potter illustrated her Peter Rabbit letter with drawings of the rabbit family, of Mr. McGregor wielding his rake, of the cabbages in the garden and of Peter tucked into bed on his return home. Sometimes drawings make things clearer and sometimes they are just for fun. Grab a pencil or some felts. Check out the graphics on your computer. Rubber stamps and stickers are also good.

Letter Writing TIP #6 • Say what you are feeling

Letters are a great place to get things off your chest. Whining on paper is often preferable to live-action whining.

L.M. Montgomery, writing to her friend in Alberta, has a little moan about housework, saying that four days of cleaning has made her feel as though all the dirt she has stirred up has stuck itself to her soul.

THINGS TO WHINE ABOUT

People to Write

Over the course of his lifetime Lewis Carroll wrote more than 100,000 letters. It was not unusual for him to write thirteen letters a day.

Ahlberg, Allan and Janet. *The Jolly Postman.*

Open the envelopes and snoop at the mail of the witch, the big bad wolf, the three little pigs and other inhabitants of the world of fairy tale and nursery rhyme.

Asch, Frank and Vladimir Vagin. *Dear Brother.*

Brothers Joey and Marvin find a cache of letters in their attic — letters between their great-great-granduncles. We snoop at the letters along with the boys and discover some goofy and sad stories of brothers long ago. What makes this book odd and funny is that all the characters are mice.

Cleary, Beverly. *Dear Mr. Henshaw.*

Leigh Botts starts writing to author Boyd Henshaw as a school assignment but one letter leads to another and soon Leigh is letting Mr. Henshaw and us into the important things in his life — his loneliness in a new school, his triumph over the lunch box thief, his anger at the broken promises of his absent father. In the course of this correspondence, Leigh turns into a real writer.

Hesse, Karen. *Letters from Rifka.*

Rifka writes these letters to her cousin in the margins of a book of poetry. She cannot send them because her family is on the run, escaping from Russia to a new life in America. Hunger, loneliness, fear, sickness, bravery, humor and the kindness of strangers. Based on a real-life family story.

Lyons, Mary E. *Letters from a Slave Girl: The Story of Harriet Jacobs.*

Harriet, an escaping slave, writes letters to her dead mother and others in the margins of an old account book. Through these letters we learn of her loneliness, hiding out for seven years in a garret cut off from her family, and of her eventual heroic triumph. The letters are invented but Harriet's story actually happened.

Major, Kevin. *Dear Bruce Springsteen.*

Get a guitar. Get a band. Get a girlfriend. What better way to deal with a life where Dad has flown the coop and Mom has a new boyfriend? And who better to tell than Bruce Springsteen? Fourteen-year-old Terry sorts things out in a series of letters to his hero.

Marsden, John. *Letters from the Inside.*
Mandy and Tracey connect through
a pen-pal ad. At first their letters
deal with regular pen-pal stuff —
school, brothers, sports, music. But
there come to be odd details in
Tracey's letters, things don't add up.
Tracey obviously has a secret, possi-
bly a sad and dangerous one, but
what is it? Can friendship survive
based on illusion?

Potter, Beatrix. *Dear Peter Rabbit.*
A selection of Potter's miniature letters, originally written to children,
are woven into this story of Peter
and his friends.

Ware, Cheryl. *Sea Monkey Summer.*
In the summer between grades six
and seven Venola Mae Cutright
gets a job, opens a bank account,
cures her plantar warts with magic,
exposes a consumer scam, fails to
identify some criminals and decides
to be cremated. We learn about
these events in Venola's hilarious
letters to her friend at camp, her
boss, and Dear Abby.

Webster, Jean. *Daddy-Long-Legs.*
Judy is an orphan. She gets the surprise of her life when the matron of
the orphanage tells her that a kind
rich man is going to pay for her
college education. All he requires is
that Judy write him regular letters.
Not knowing his name, Judy writes
to her benefactor as "Daddy-Long-
Legs." But who is the real recipient?
The identity of Daddy-Long-Legs
gives Judy the second big surprise
of her life.

Williams, Vera, with illustrations by
Jennifer Williams. *Stringbean's Trip to
the Shining Sea.*
When Stringbean and his brother
take off in a truck for a summer on
the road, they record their adventures in a set of postcards home.
The search for the circus clown, the
ghost horse, the lizard adoption —
reading these postcards makes you
wish you had been along on the
trip.

Write While You Sleep

One night writer Susan Cooper had a dream. In the dream she was standing on the roof of a building at dawn. Around her was a golden city and, in one direction, a park with spreading green trees. She wanted to go to that park but she could not see how to climb down from the roof. She touched a golden railing, which fell away with a clang and became a ladder. She climbed down the ladder and came to a stone staircase. She ran down it, faster and faster, heading for the trees.

At this point, Susan Cooper woke up. But before the dream faded, she grabbed a pencil and wrote it down.

In many ways, this dream is a lot like a story. It has a setting, time and place. It has details to make us feel that we are there — colors, texture and sound. Most of all, it has emotion — wonder, joy, trepidation, excitement and desire.

Some weeks later, Susan Cooper, who was writing a fantasy novel called *Silver on the Tree* (the fifth and final book of her *Dark Is Rising* series), remembered her beautiful and mysterious dream. She expanded it and incorporated it into her adventure. In one of the most memorable scenes in the book, her two characters, Will and Bran, are transported to a golden place called the Lost Land. From a high roof, they look out over a great city, and then they climb down a ladder that magically appears.

Dreams feel absolutely real when we are inside them. Susan Cooper captures this feeling of concrete reality in her fantasy writing. We know the Lost Land — its colors, sounds, smells. And we feel what the boys are feeling — excitement and fear.

Dreams

DREAMS SWEET AND STRANGE

Some people believe that dreams contain messages about the future. Some believe that dreams are communications from

other worlds, from other beings or the dead. Other people think dreams are a kind of code that can be translated. Or that dreams tell us important things about our true selves.

One thing is for sure: when we dream, we are all writers. We are creating original imaginary worlds. We are taking all the stuff that is in our heads and rearranging it to make something that nobody else could

have made. And it takes no effort. It is all free for the taking, waiting for us under our pillows every night.

Dreams give us pictures — a keyboard that produces three-dimensional wooden letters as you type, a tiny man with a human body and butterfly wings, bedsheets with glued-on Smarties.

Dreams give us new selves to try on — a fearless public-speaking self, a shiny and muscular body-builder self, a flying self, a rock star self.

And dreams give us powerful feelings — the panic of stepping onto a carpet that turns to quicksand, the frustration of trying to buy a ticket for the circus and all the ticket seller will give you is three eggs, the exhilaration of swooping down a gravel hill while sitting on a suitcase, the horror of a baby that is only a head.

Dreams start fading away the moment we wake up. Sometimes all that is left is the feeling. Writing down your dreams helps capture them. It also becomes easier to remember your dreams if you start recording them.

Keeping a dream journal has two big advantages for a writer. First of all, you don't have to think about what to write. Your subconscious has already done all the work. Second, dreams give you lots of good stuff. Perhaps you will never use a dream as directly as Susan Cooper did, but

there will be something to enrich your writing — an image, a character, a setting, a question, a feeling. Dreams are a gift for everyone — especially for writers.

Robert Louis Stevenson suffered horribly from nightmares. He describes waking up "screaming and in the extremest frenzy of terror." His father would come into his room and make up soothing stories about talking to the mailman until Louis could calm down.

> "The pages come alive under my fingertips, which is a wonderful exhilarating feeling. It is the reason for writing. When you have had that feeling once, you never forget it."
> Martin Waddell

> "All I can tell you is that pictures come into my head and I write stories about them."
> C.S. Lewis

> "Everyone has a story.
> Once you start, the
> possibilities are endless."
> Michael Kusugak

Carroll, Lewis. *Alice's Adventures in Wonderland.*

In the most well-known literary dream of all time, Alice falls asleep on a hot summer afternoon and enters Wonderland, an elaborate and curious world as weird and real as only dreams can be.

Dickinson, Peter, with illustrations by Alan Cober. *Giant Cold.*

A boy, holidaying with his parents on a tropical island, has a dream in which he shrinks, is put on display as an elf-child, escapes on the back of a bird and walks inside the ear of Giant Cold. Like a dream this book keeps you going, just to find out what happens.

Jarrell, Randall, with illustrations by Maurice Sendak. *Fly by Night.*

"At night David can fly. In the day-time he can't. In the daytime, he doesn't even remember that he can." When David is night flying he can see the dreams of his parents, his dog, a herd of sheep, and he can hear the animals talking, the conversations of mice and a mother owl telling a bedtime story. Is this a book about dreaming or not?

London, Jonathan, with illustrations by G. Brian Karas. *Into This Night We Are Rising.*

In this dream journey the children float, fly and sail through a sky of cloud pillow fights, music, friendly dragons and animals in the stars. This is more like a poem than a story. A few simple words, carefully chosen, can take you to another world.

Rylant, Cynthia, with illustrations by Barry Moser. *The Dreamer.*

From daydreams and night dreams the artist creates a whole world and lives in it. But who is this artist?

Van Allsburg, Chris. *Ben's Dream.*

If you meet a friend in a dream is that friend really there? No, it's just your dream. But what if the friend also has the dream and sees you? This is the puzzle of this story of two friends who float away in a flood.

Van Allsburg, Chris. *The Sweetest Fig.*

Monsieur Bibot the dentist receives two figs that make his dreams come true. After the first fig he ends up in public without his trousers, so he tries to hypnotize himself into dreams of wealth. It doesn't quite work out.